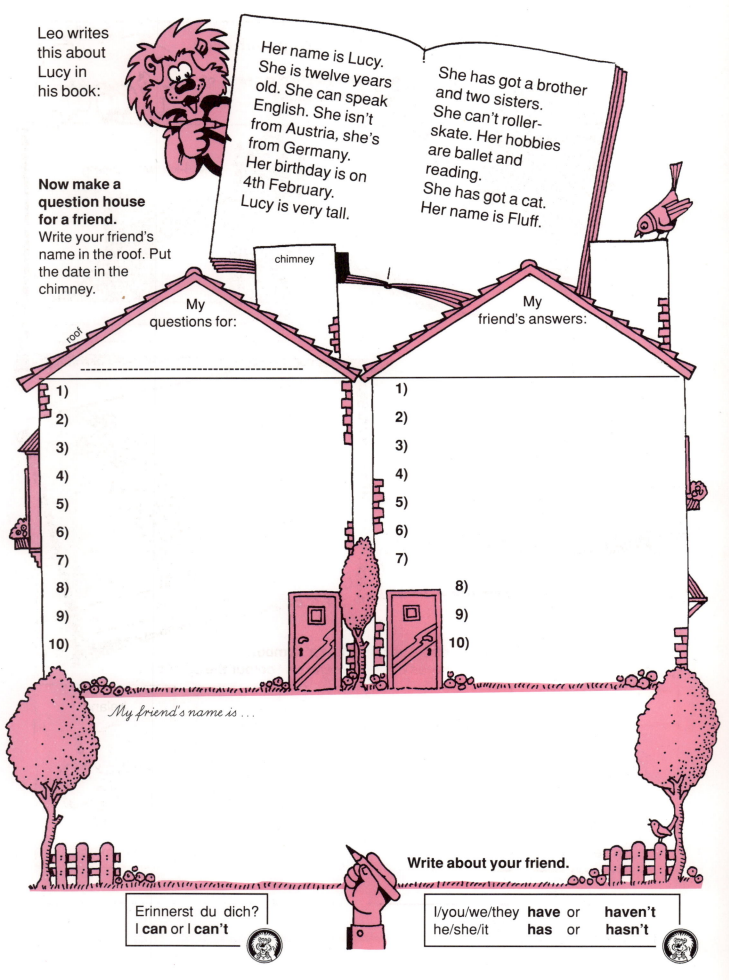

Read about a school day

I'm Lucy. I always get up at half past seven. I go to the bathroom before my sister Sally. She never gets up early. Then I put on my school uniform and have breakfast in the kitchen. I usually eat muesli for breakfast and I drink cocoa or orange juice.

I'm Tim. We have lessons all morning until one o'clock, and then we have our lunch break. Most of my friends eat a hot snack at school or bring sandwiches with them from home. Pupils at British schools have lessons every afternoon, too. At my school we finish at four o'clock in the afternoon. I'm in the basketball team, so I often stay at school to practise for an hour before I go home. After dinner I do my homework and then I sometimes watch TV before I go to bed.

I'm Janet. Lucy and I are in the same class at school. I meet Lucy at 8.15 and we go to school together. We usually go by bike, but in winter my father often takes us to school by car. School starts at quarter to nine.

What do most British pupils wear?

Right (✓) or wrong (x)?

	✓	x
Lucy gets up at 7.30.	S	A
Sally goes to the bathroom first.	E	C
Lucy wears jeans at school.	G	H
She likes muesli for breakfast.	O	F
Janet meets Lucy at quarter to eight.	K	O
They sometimes go to school by car.	L	M
Lessons at Tim's school finish at 2 o'clock.	P	U
Tim and his friends go home for lunch.	R	N
Not many pupils have lessons in the afternoon.	T	I
Tim usually plays basketball after school.	F	S
Tim has dinner at school.	W	O
He does his homework before dinner.	U	R
He never watches TV.	Y	M

Richtig (✓) oder falsch (x)? Wenn du richtig entschieden hast, entsteht aus den markierten Buchstaben das Lösungswort.

Fill in:

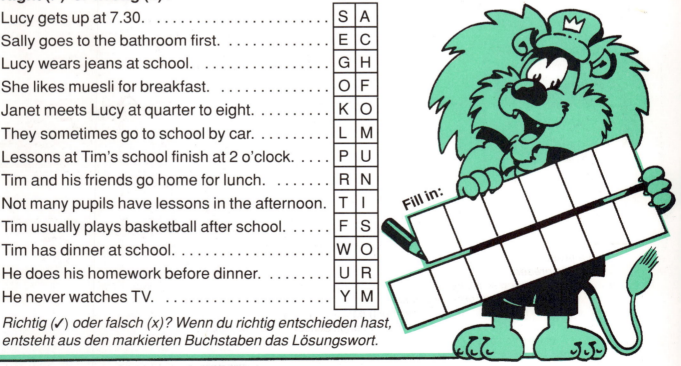

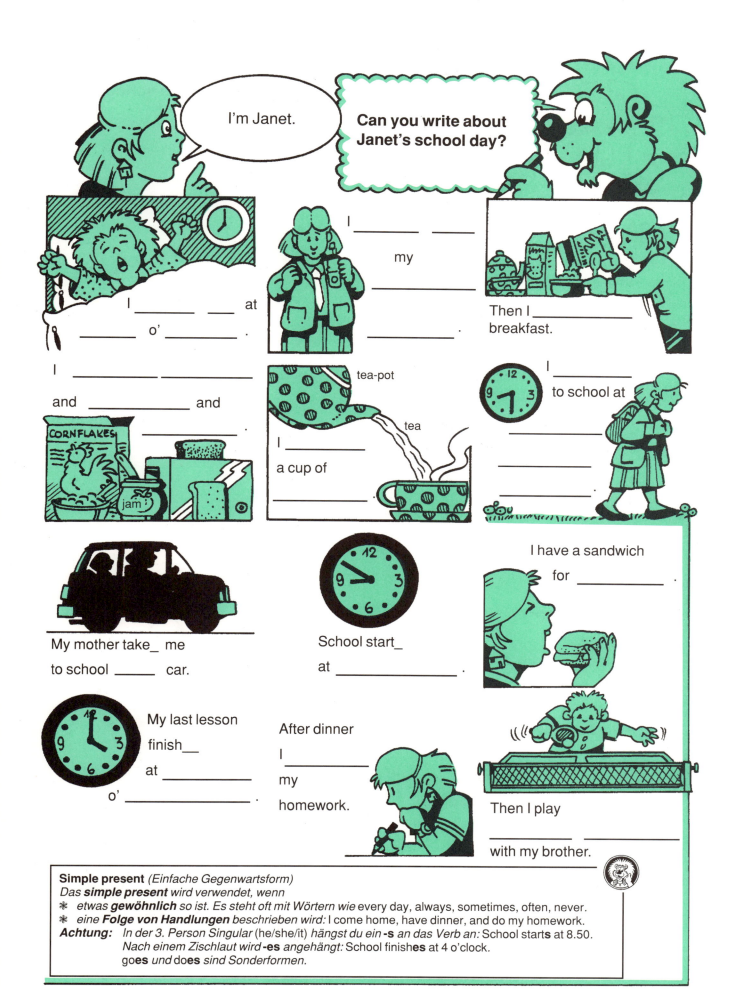

Fragesätze im simple present bildest du
mit dem Hilfsverb **to do** und der **Grundform des Verbs**.
Do I/you/we/they **speak** English? **Does** he/she/it **live** in Australia?

Die **Verneinung im simple present** bildest du
mit dem Hilfsverb **to do** + **not** + **der Grundform des Verbs**.
I **do not** (= don't) **watch** TV. – He **does not** (=doesn't) **watch** TV.

Can I ask you a few questions, please?

Thank you very much.

teacher's family name: Mr./Mrs./Miss _____

Now ask your English teacher.

questions

What's your first name, please?

Do you get up early every morning?

Do you have muesli for breakfast?

What's your favourite colour?

Do you go to school by bus?

Do you speak French?

Have you got a pet?

Is your birthday in summer?

Do you smoke cigarettes?

Can you play the guitar?

Do you often watch TV?

answers

Put in the right word: do, does, don't, doesn't

Peter is sitting at the breakfast table. He _____ feel hungry this morning.

"_____ you want some toast and marmalade?" his mother asks.

"No thanks, Mum. I feel ill," replies Peter.

"Well, I _____ think you can go to school today," his mother says.

Peter is very pleased. He isn't really ill, but he can't find his English books.

"_____ your teacher want to test your English today?" his mother asks.

"I _____ know!" Peter answers and he smiles. "Why _____ you ask?"

How _____ Mother know the real reason?

"_____ you want to stay in bed the whole day, Peter?" his mother asks.

But Peter _____ like this idea. He wants to play football this afternoon.

"No, I feel better already, Mum," he says.

Take the last letter and put it into the box.

Example: He doesn't feel hungry this morning.

| w | | h | i | | l | e | s | f | r | | m | | c | | l | a | n | d |

Neue Ensslin-Englischspiele 2

9*

Look at this word puzzle. **Can you find the plural of these words?** Draw a line through the word.

~~dog~~ – hobby – skirt – shoe – pen – foot – pet – tooth – key – child – rose – pony – cow – apple – church – boy – sandwich – knife – mouse – tomato – man – newspaper – fish – woman – sausage

Some words go across →,

some words go down ↓,

some words go diagonally ↘.

```
S H O B B I E S L U R T
S A N D W I C H E S A O
L W U C H U R C H E S M
N E W S P A P E R S O A
C O W S A E P E K R D T
H S A R K G T P N E E O
I V P O N I E S L S Y E
L E R Y I E M S M E N S
D O G S V A I S F I S H
R W O M E N C T E E T H
E B O Y S Y E R O S E S
N S H O E S K I R T S T
```

There are 21 letters left. Can you find the sentence? Leo says:

P _ _ _ _ _ _ _ _ _ _ _ _ _ _ _ _ _ _ _ _ _ .

Now finish these sentences with the right plural word from the puzzle.

"My teacher has got big _____!"
Susan's pets are two white _____.
Please clean your _____ twice a day.
Our milk comes from _____.
_____ are red. You can eat them.
_____ are smaller than horses.
_____ often play football.
I need a new pair of black _____.
_____ often wear earrings.
You need _____ to make "hot dogs"!
_____ are very pretty flowers.
There are four _____ in our town.
partners: _____ and forks
Sam's _____ are football and judo.
"I need my _____ to open these doors."
I often eat _____ at school.
Little _____ play with toys.

10*

Neue Ensslin-Englischspiele 2

A visit to a safari park

Can you complete the sentences? Use the present simple or present progressive form.

① Dad, some monkeys _____ (sit) on our car. They often _____ (jump) onto cars.

② Look, they _____ to the next car now. (go)

③ Help! What _____ that elephant _____ ? (do)

④ It _____ (look) for an apple.

⑤ _____ tourists often _____ the animals? (feed) No, visitors mustn't feed the animals.

⑥ Why _____ that wolf _____ behind a tree? (hide)

A lot of animals _____ _____ visitors. (not/like)

⑦ That giraffe _____ (watch) us. It looks hungry. But giraffes never _____ people. (eat)

⑧ These lions _____ for their food. (wait) I'm hungry, too. Let's have a picnic.

⑨ _____ zebras _____ picnics, too? (like)

Good evening.

Here is the Six o'Clock News.

There was a very bad earthquake in Indiana last night. 5,000 people died and 20,000 people lost their homes. The Red Cross sent help to the area immediately.

earthquake: *Erdbeben*
area: *Gebiet*

A mountain rescue team helped two climbers in Wales this morning. The climbers left yesterday afternoon to climb Mount Snowdon. There was thick fog and they lost their way. So they spent the night on the mountain. They were cold and hungry when the rescue team found them.

fog: *Nebel*
mountain rescue team: *Gebirgsrettungsmannschaft*
climber: *Bergsteiger*
Mount Snowdon: *höchster Berg in Wales*

Simple past *(Einfache Vergangenheitsform)*
Wenn du über einen Vorgang sprichst, der in der Vergangenheit stattgefunden hat und vollkommen abgeschlossen ist, dann benutze das **simple past**. *Der Zeitpunkt oder der Zeitraum der Handlung wird oft durch Zeitangaben benannt wie:* yesterday, last week, three years ago, in 1970.
Susan visit**ed** her grandmother **yesterday**.
Du bildest das simple past aus der **Grundform des Verbs** + **-ed**: visit**ed**, help**ed**.
Achtung! -y nach einem Konsonanten wird zu -ie-: cry ⇨ cri**ed**.
Unregelmäßige Formen wie lose ⇨ lost; am/is ⇨ was; are ⇨ were; spend ⇨ spent *mußt du dir merken.*

Now you try! Write your news here.

_____
_____
_____
_____
_____

Find the past tense of these verbs. (Look at the news on page 14.)

- lose _____
- is _____
- spend _____
- send _____
- leave _____
- are _____
- help _____
- find _____
- die _____

snail: _Schnecke_

Join the German words to the right snail.

finden – helfen – verbringen – ist – sind – schicken – sterben – fortgehen – verlieren

Can you finish these sentences?

Where **did** a mountain rescue team **help** two climbers? – The team _____ climbers _____ .

When _____ the climbers _____ ? – They left yesterday afternoon.

Did they **know** their way down again? – No, they _____ _____ their way.

Where _____ they _____ the night? – They spent the night on the mountain.

Die Frageform des **simple past** _bildest du in der Regel mit_ **did** + **Grundform des Verbs**.
Did you **climb** the mountain yesterday?

Die Verneinung des **simple past** _bildest du mit_ **didn't** _und der Grundform_.
They **didn't** climb the mountain.

Neue Ensslin-Englischspiele 2

Who went on holiday?

Wer fuhr in Urlaub?

"go went ..."

- Did you go to Scotland?
- No, I didn't. I went to France.
- Did you go to France, too?
- Yes, I did.

Now you try.

Where did you go on holiday? *I went to ...*

Where did you stay? *I stayed in ...*

What did you do? _____

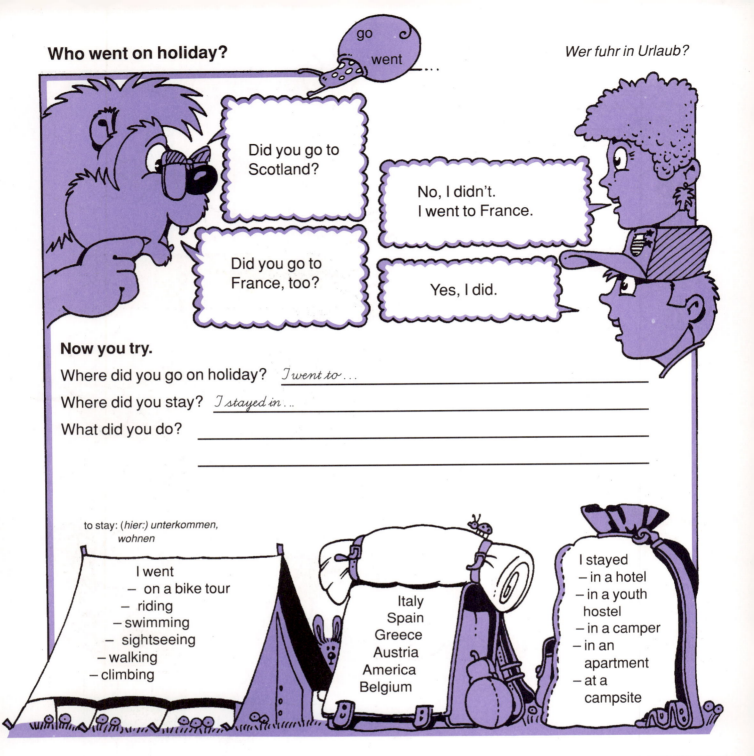

to stay: (*hier:*) unterkommen, wohnen

I went
– on a bike tour
– riding
– swimming
– sightseeing
– walking
– climbing

Italy
Spain
Greece
Austria
America
Belgium

I stayed
– in a hotel
– in a youth hostel
– in a camper
– in an apartment
– at a campsite

Stick a holiday photo here.

*Wenn das **Fragewort** gleichzeitig **Subjekt** des Fragesatzes ist, formulierst du die Frage **ohne** do/does/did.*
Who went on holiday? (who = *Subjekt: wer*)
What happened in India? (what = *Subjekt: was*)

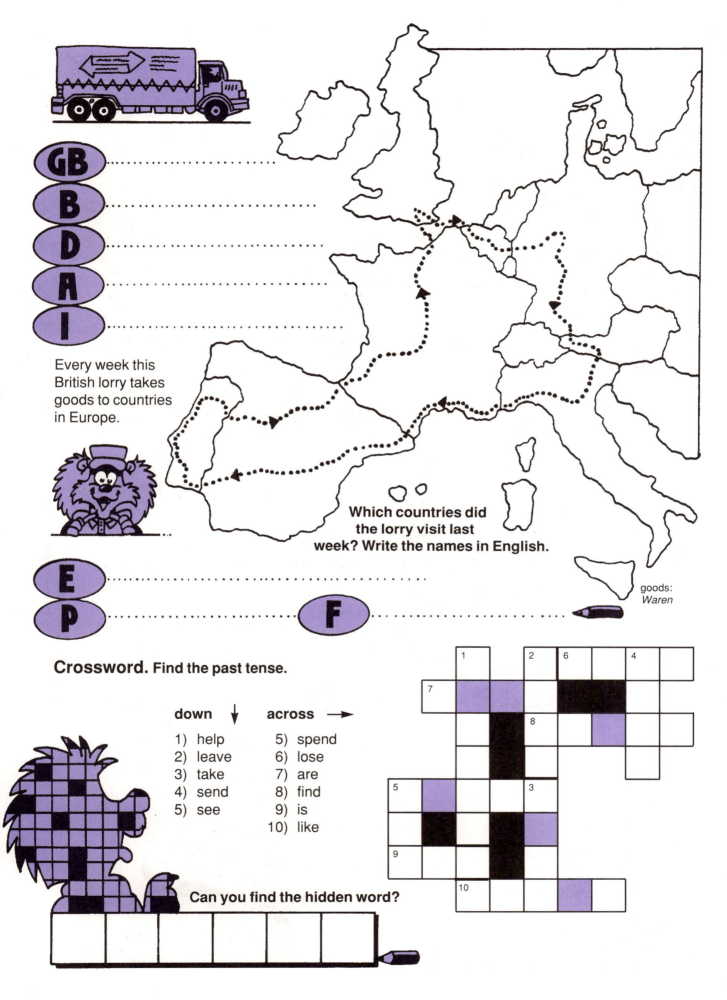

GB ....
B ....
D ....
A ....
I ....

Every week this British lorry takes goods to countries in Europe.

E ....
P ....   **F** ....

Which countries did the lorry visit last week? Write the names in English.

goods: *Waren*

Crossword. Find the past tense.

down ↓
1) help
2) leave
3) take
4) send
5) see

across →
5) spend
6) lose
7) are
8) find
9) is
10) like

Can you find the hidden word?

The first "Modern Men" to live in Britain.

Forty thousand years ago there was still ice over most of Britain. Small groups of hunters lived in the south of England. They looked for shelter in caves. One of these caves is Kent's Cavern, near Torquay on the south-west coast of England. Generations of hunters lived here for over 20,000 years, and these clever men were the first Modern Men to live in Britain. The cave goes over 100 metres into the limestone hill. You can see lots of stalactites there.

The hunters used tools of flint, antler and bone. They made clothes of fur and knew how to use fire. Present-day explorers found parts of mammoths, rhinoceroses, bears, horses and other animals in the cave.

mammoth

limestone hill: *Kalksteinhügel*

stalactite

cave: *Höhle*

fire

rhinoceros

to use: *benutzen*
shelter: *Schutz*
present-day explorer: *Forscher von heute*

flint: *Feuerstein*
antler: *Geweih*
bone: *Knochen*

tools = *Werkzeug*

hunter: *Jäger*

fur: *Fell*

know / knew

True or false?
1) 40,000 years ago it was very hot in England. _____
2) The first "Modern Men" were very clever. _____
3) They lived in modern houses. _____

A mammoth is a prehistoric animal. On this page you can stick in two pictures of prehistoric animals.

animal's name: *stegosaurus*

when did it live? *250 million years ago*

what did it look like? *It looked very fierce.*

what did it eat? *It ate plants.*

more information: *It weighed about two tonnes, but it had a very small brain (only as big as a golf ball).*

animal's name: _____

when did it live? _____

what did it look like? _____

what did it eat? _____

more information: _____
_____

animal's name _____

when did it live? _____

what did it look like? _____

what did it eat? _____

more information: _____
_____

to weigh: *wiegen*	to look like: *aussehen wie*
brain: *Gehirn*	2 years ago: *vor 2 Jahren*
fierce: *wild*	

Neue Ensslin-Englischspiele 2

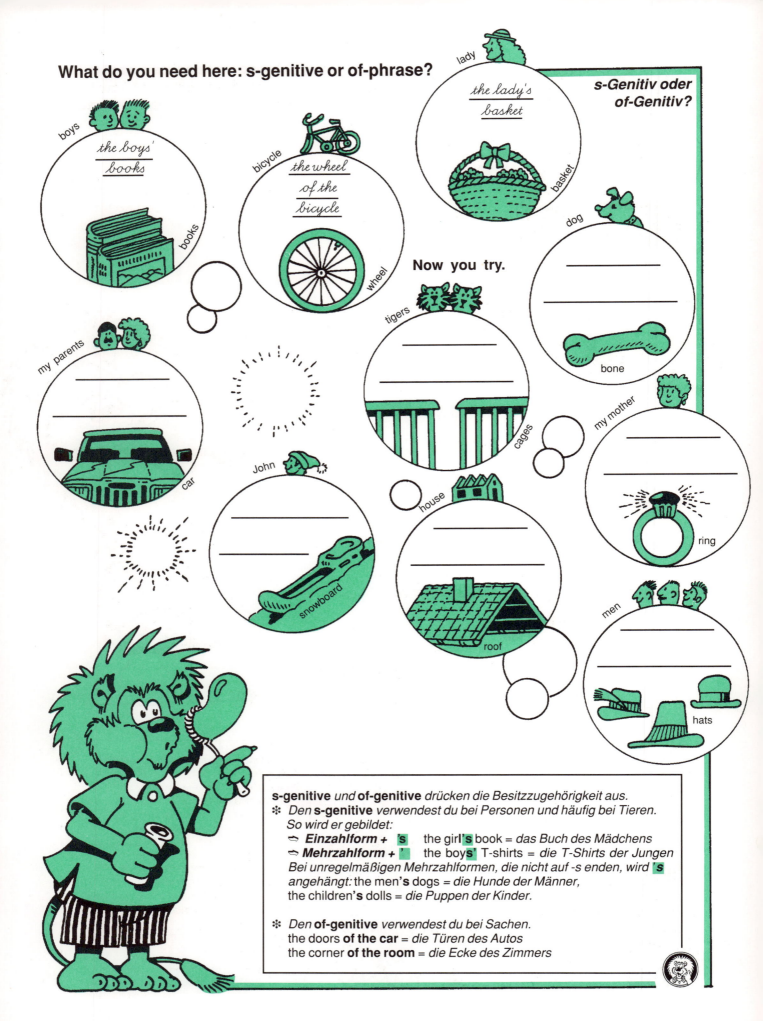

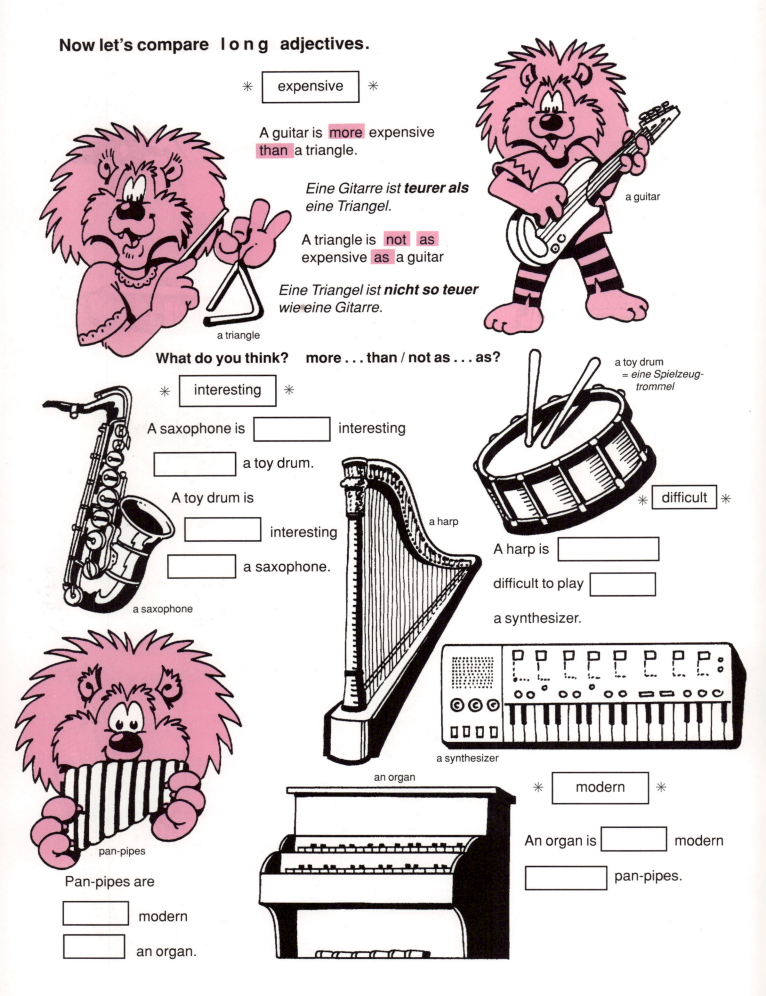

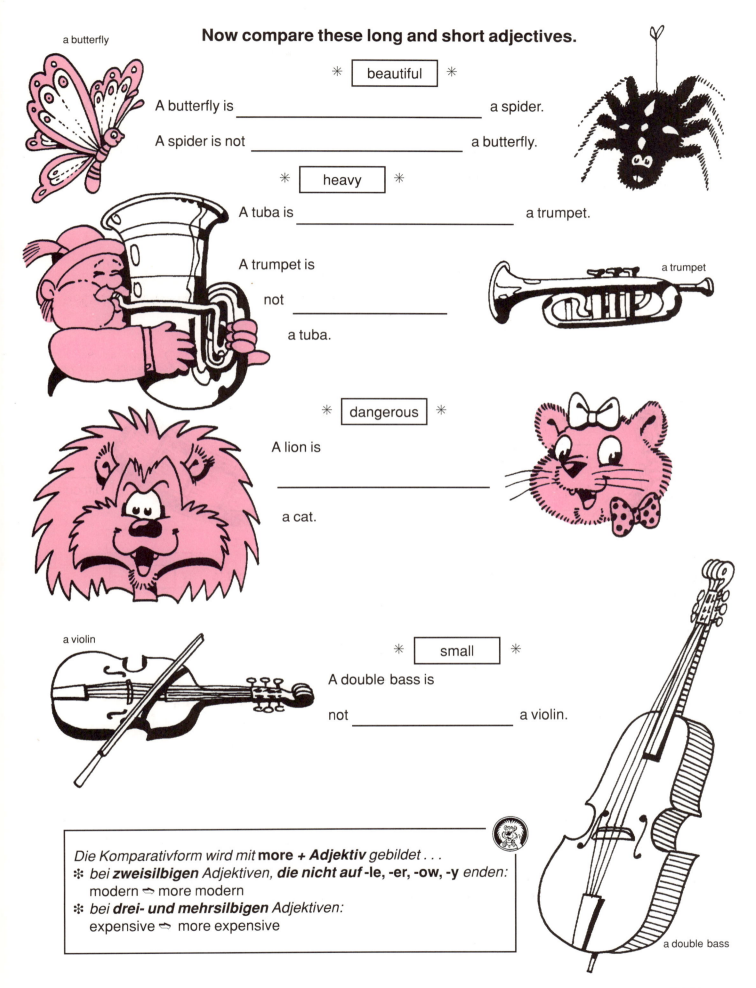

Now compare these long and short adjectives.

✴ beautiful ✴

A butterfly is _____ a spider.

A spider is not _____ a butterfly.

✴ heavy ✴

A tuba is _____ a trumpet.

A trumpet is not _____ a tuba.

✴ dangerous ✴

A lion is _____ a cat.

✴ small ✴

A double bass is not _____ a violin.

*Die Komparativform wird mit **more + Adjektiv** gebildet ...*
✲ *bei **zweisilbigen** Adjektiven, **die nicht auf** -le, -er, -ow, -y enden:*
  modern ⇨ more modern
✲ *bei **drei- und mehrsilbigen** Adjektiven:*
  expensive ⇨ more expensive

Superlatives *Superlative*

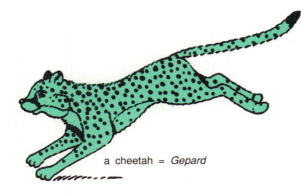

a cheetah = *Gepard*

A cheetah is the **fastest** animal on earth.

London is the **most famous** city in England.

What do you think?

_____ is the _____ mountain
                  (high)
in _____ .

M _ r _ _ _ _ is
the _____ planet.
     (hot)

Mercury: *Merkur*

_____ is the _____ tunnel
                             (long)
in _____ .

Now make superlatives with words from the box. ↓

_____ is the ☐ ☐ German car.
_____ is the ☐ ☐ person in America.
_____ is the ☐ ☐ subject at school.
_____ is the ☐ ☐ animal.

| famous |
| dangerous |
| difficult |
| expensive |

> *Den* **Superlativ** *bildest du aus . . .*
> * **Adjektiv** + **-est**, *wenn der regelmäßige Komparativ auf* -er *endet,*
>   long ⇨ long**er** ⇨ the long**est**
>   = *lang* ⇨ *länger* ⇨ *der/die/das längste*
> * **most** + **Adjektiv**, *wenn der Komparativ mit* **more** *gebildet wird.*
>   expensive ⇨ more expensive ⇨ the most expensive
>   = *teuer* ⇨ *teurer* ⇨ *der/die/das teuerste*
> *Beachte* **unregelmäßige Steigerungen** *wie*
> good ⇨ better ⇨ best – bad ⇨ worse ⇨ worst

Look what Chris Harris did this Saturday.

8.30 – 9.00 had breakfast

9.15 – 11.15 played football

12.00 – 12.30 had lunch

12.30 – 1.30 listened to CDs

hutch = *Kaninchenstall*

2.00 – 3.00 cleaned his rabbit's hutch

3.30 – 4.00 wrote a letter to his pen-friend

Now say what Chris was doing at these times.

At 8.45 *he was having breakfast.*   At 1 o'clock _____

At 11 o'clock _____   At 2.30 _____

At 12.15 _____   At 3.45 _____

Das **past progressive** *wird mit der* **Vergangenheitsform von** to be *und der* **-ing-Form** *des Verbs gebildet:* At 8.45 Chris **was having** breakfast. = *Um 8.45 Uhr frühstückte Chris gerade.*

What was happening here? Complete the sentences. Use the past tense.

Mother _____ (read) a book when the telephone _____ (ring).

Jo _____ (fall) off the ladder while he _____ (paint) the kitchen ceiling.

We _____ (wait) for the bus when we _____ (see) an accident.

Wenn ein Vorgang gerade ablief und währenddessen eine neue Handlung dazukam, benutzt man für die **Hintergrundhandlung** *das* **past progressive** *und für die* **neu eintretende Handlung** *das* **simple past**: They **were playing** tennis, when it **began** to rain. = *Sie spielten gerade Tennis, als es zu regnen begann.*

Ein Wortschatzspiel für 2 bis 4 Personen

Jeder Spieler braucht 6 leere Kärtchen aus Papier oder Pappe, einen Stift und eine Spielfigur. Ihr braucht auch einen Würfel. Und so wird's gemacht: Jeder sucht aus dem Vokabelteil dieses Buches (ab Seite 62) 6 Wörter aus und schreibt sie auf seine Kärtchen – englisch auf eine Seite, deutsch auf die andere Seite. Zeigt eure Wörter nicht den anderen Spielern!

Nun werden die Kärtchen aller Spieler zusammengemischt und mit der deutschen Seite nach oben neben das Spielfeld gelegt. Stellt die Spielfiguren auf das Startfeld. Der jüngste Mitspieler fängt an und würfelt. Er darf so viele Felder vorgehen, wie er Würfelaugen hat. Zeigt der Würfel eine 3, 4 oder 5, nimmt der Spieler außerdem eine Wortschatzkarte. Wenn er weiß, wie das deutsche Wort auf englisch heißt, darf er 2 Plätze vorrücken. Der Spieler, der als erster bei „finish" ankommt, hat gewonnen.

Für das nächste Spiel müßt ihr neue Wortschatzkarten basteln.

Viel Spaß!

What has happened here? Use the present perfect tense.

Was ist hier geschehen?

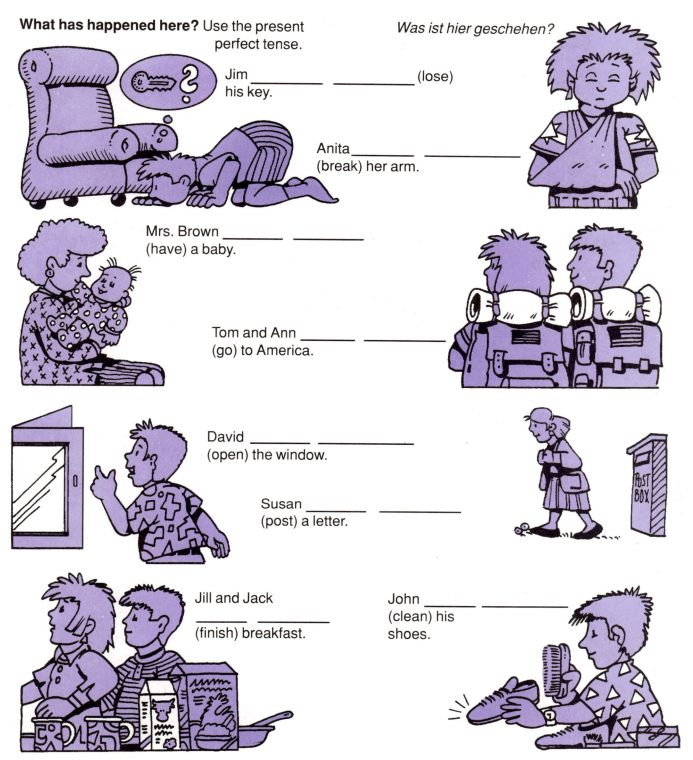

Jim _____ _____ (lose) his key.

Anita _____ _____ (break) her arm.

Mrs. Brown _____ _____ (have) a baby.

Tom and Ann _____ _____ (go) to America.

David _____ _____ (open) the window.

Susan _____ _____ (post) a letter.

Jill and Jack _____ _____ (finish) breakfast.

John _____ _____ (clean) his shoes.

past particles: open ⇨ open**ed**; finish ⇨ finish**ed**; clean ⇨ clean**ed**; lose ⇨ **lost**; break ⇨ **broken**; go ⇨ **gone**; have ⇨ **had**

---

*Das **present perfect simple** (Perfekt) bildest du mit einer Form von **to have** und dem **past participle** (Partizip Perfekt) des Verbs.*
*Das past participle besteht in der Regel aus der **Grundform des Verbs** + **-ed**. Aber es gibt viele unregelmäßige Formen (broken, lost, gone . . .).*
*Benutze das **present perfect**, wenn du ausdrücken willst, daß eine Handlung in der Vergangenheit stattfand, aber immer noch ein wirksames Ergebnis in der Gegenwart hat.*
Mother has gone shopping. (⇨ Mutter ist beim Einkaufen. Sie ist noch nicht wieder zurück.)
*In Sätzen mit dem **present perfect simple** benutze **keine** Zeitangaben der Vergangenheit (z. B. last, yesterday, ago).*
*John **has cleaned** his shoes **today**. (present perfect) / He **didn't clean** them **yesterday**. (simple past)*

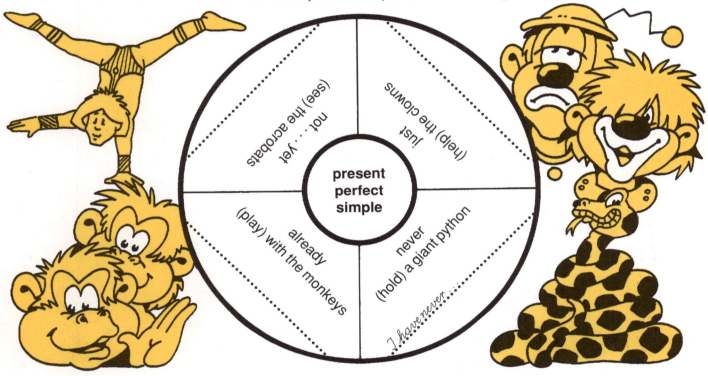

Mit dem **present perfect simple** benutzt man oft: **ever** (jemals), **never** (noch nie), **not . . . yet** (noch nicht), **just** (gerade), **already** (schon).
Wortstellung: I have **never** sat on an elephant.   I have **already** given the horses some water.
               Have you **ever** fed the tigers?   I have**n't** done my homework **yet**.

Now ask questions with ever:

Have you _____ (watch) the lion trainer?

Have _____ (jump) on the trampoline?

Can you find the past tense and the past participle forms of these irregular verbs?

break - broke - broken
lose -
go -
have -
feed -
do -
sit -
win -
give -
hold -
see -

Now write about the circus workshop. Use the **past tense**.
Say what you did and what you didn't do.

Yesterday I

What has happened this month?
Use the **present perfect tense.**

In your family:

At your school:

In your country:

In the world:

Leo and his friends are camping in one of farmer Elliot's fields. **What have they been doing this afternoon?**
Use the **present perfect progressive**.

(pick flowers)

(talk to farmer Elliot)

(do the washing-up)

from the farm-house.
(fetch water)

(write letters)

(cook sausages)

(collect wood)

(repair my bike)

Das **present perfect progressive** bildest du aus dem **present perfect** von **to be** (has/have been) und der **-ing-Form** des Verbs:
I **have been doing** my homework.

Das **present perfect progressive** drückt aus, daß ein **Vorgang in der Vergangenheit** begann und

❋ ***bis in die Gegenwart anhält*** oder   ❋ ***soeben zu Ende gegangen ist.***

I have been writing letters. – Ich habe gerade Briefe geschrieben. (Ich bin auch noch dabei.)

32*

Neue Ensslin-Englischspiele 2

Save the whale!

A beautiful blue whale has lost its way and has swum onto this beach.
The girls and boys are trying to save it.
Leo has come to see them.

Use the present perfect progressive.

① John _____ _____ _____ (talk) to the newspaper reporter _____ (for/since) 10 minutes. ② The children _____ _____ _____ (wait) to see the whale go back into the sea _____ (for/since) this morning. ③ I _____ _____ _____ (look) for the other whales _____ (for/since) 2 o'clock. ④ Sheila _____ _____ _____ (talk) to the whale _____ (for/since) a long time. ⑤ We _____ _____ _____ (pour) water over the whale _____ (for/since) an hour.

What have you been doing?

Beim present perfect progressive *steht oft* **since** *oder* **for**.
✻ **since** *(seit) wird gebraucht, wenn ein* **Zeitpunkt** *angegeben wird* (3 o'clock, this morning)
✻ **for** *(seit) wird gebraucht, wenn ein* **Zeitraum** *angegeben wird* (10 minutes, 3 hours). Im Deutschen steht dann häufig Präsens + „schon".
He has been talking to Mr. X for 10 minutes. / *Er spricht schon seit 10 Minuten mit Herrn X.*

Pancake Day

Pfannkuchentag

The Christian time of fasting before Easter is called "Lent".
Lent starts in February and the first day is Ash Wednesday.
It is traditional to eat lots and lots of pancakes on the day before Ash Wednesday.
This day is called "Pancake Tuesday".
There are lots of pancake races on that day, too. People run through the streets with a pancake in a frying pan. They must toss the pancake at the beginning and at the end of the race.

Lent: *Fastenzeit*
Ash Wednesday: *Aschermittwoch*
to toss = to throw up in the air

← frying pan

Now try this:

1) Which day is called "Pancake Tuesday"? _____

2) Which month does Lent start in? _____

3) How many times must people toss the pancake in the race? _____

4) Do you like pancakes? _____

5) Can you toss a pancake? _____

6) Can you cook pancakes? If not, look at the next page!

Have a pancake party!

Rezept für 4 Personen

ingredients:

100 g flour
300 ml milk
a pinch of salt
1 egg
oil for frying
for the filling: some sugar
                  some lemon juice

This is what you do:

✻ Sieve the flour and the salt into the mixing bowl.

✻ Break the egg into a cup. Put the egg into the mixing bowl, too. Mix these ingredients with the spoon.

✻ Add 50 ml of milk and mix again.
Add another 50 ml of milk and mix again.
Add 100 ml of milk and mix again.
Add the last 100 ml of milk and mix again.

✻ Beat the mixture with a whisk until it is smooth.

✻ Leave the mixture for 30 minutes.
It is then thicker.

✻ Put a little oil into the frying pan.
Turn on the stove.
Put the frying pan on the stove for 2 minutes.

BE CAREFUL NOW!

→→→→→ please turn over →→→→→

Have a pancake party! (page 2)

to stir: *umrühren*
to spread: *verteilen*
to loosen: *lockern*

✻ Stir the mixture. Put 4 tablespoons of the mixture into the frying pan. Spread the mixture carefully.

✻ Cook the pancake for about 2 minutes.

✻ Loosen the pancake with the scraper. Shake the frying pan and try to toss the pancake!

✻ Cook the other side for 2 minutes. Put the pancake on a plate. Put sugar and lemon juice on top. Roll the pancake up. Put some more sugar on top.

✻ Now make some more pancakes!

Can you find the words?   Write the German words here:

G S A U R = s _____ r = Zu _____ r

G E N S I I N R T E D = i _____ s = Zu _____ n

R U F O L = f _____ r = M _____ l

I V E E S = s _____ e = S _____ b

Y R F G N I A P N = f _____ p _____ = Br _____ e

Q I T E E U N M P = e _____ t = G _____ t

O M H T O S = s _____ h = gl _____ t

H K W S I = w _____ k = Sch _____ n

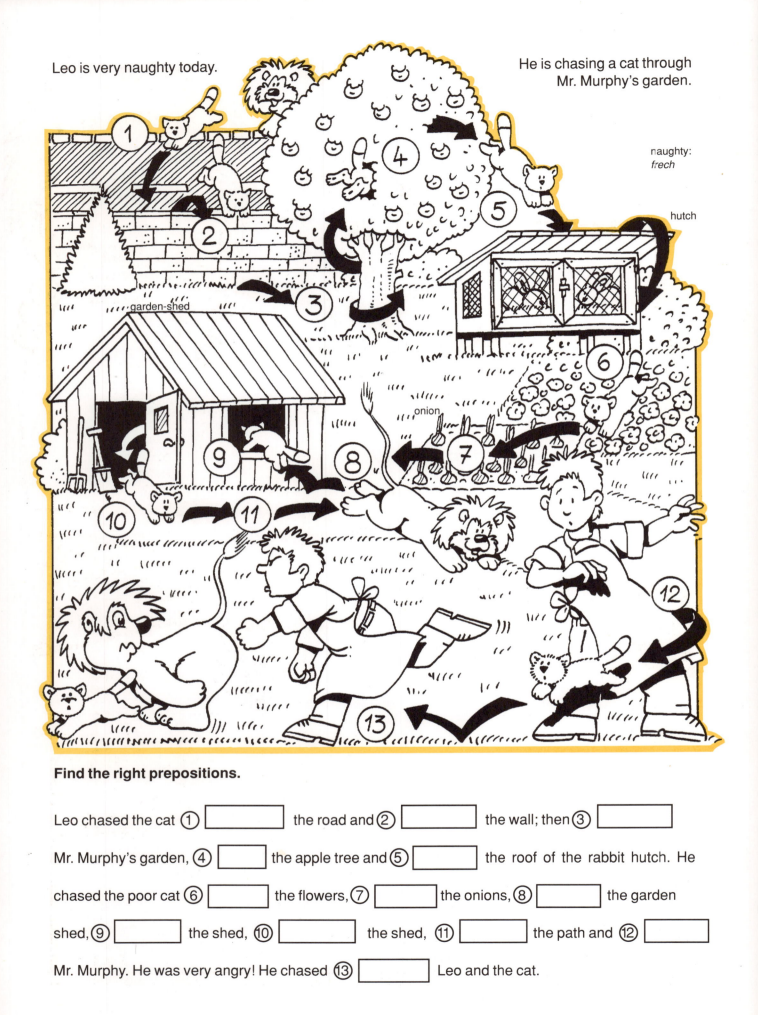

Leo is very naughty today.

He is chasing a cat through Mr. Murphy's garden.

naughty: *frech*

hutch

Find the right prepositions.

Leo chased the cat ① ▢ the road and ② ▢ the wall; then ③ ▢ Mr. Murphy's garden, ④ ▢ the apple tree and ⑤ ▢ the roof of the rabbit hutch. He chased the poor cat ⑥ ▢ the flowers, ⑦ ▢ the onions, ⑧ ▢ the garden shed, ⑨ ▢ the shed, ⑩ ▢ the shed, ⑪ ▢ the path and ⑫ ▢ Mr. Murphy. He was very angry! He chased ⑬ ▢ Leo and the cat.

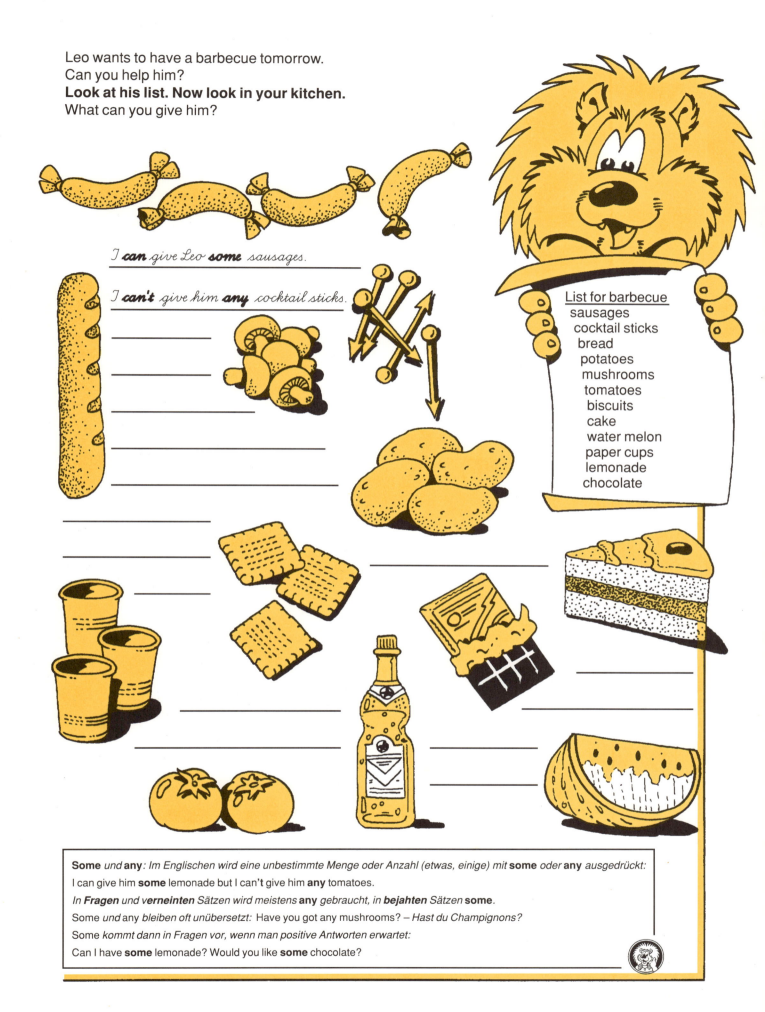

This is a story about a tramp. His name is Sam.

Look at the words on Sam's bag. Fill the gaps in the story with these words.

Sam is wearing _____ very old clothes. He hasn't got _____ money for new clothes. He doesn't live in a house and he hasn't got a job. At night he usually sleeps _____ in a park.

He puts old newspapers round him to keep warm.

Other tramps ask, "Have you got _____ to drink?"

Sam always replies, "I haven't got _____ whisky. _____ stole it."

He has still got _____ cigarettes in his bag, but he hasn't got _____ to eat.

Zusammensetzungen mit **some** *verwendest du in bejahten Sätzen.*
somebody/someone: *jemand* – something: *etwas* – somewhere: *irgendwo*
Zusammensetzungen mit **any** *verwendest du meist in Fragesätzen und verneinten Sätzen.*
not . . . anyone/anybody: *niemand* – not . . . anything: *nichts* – not . . . anywhere: *nirgends*

Early one morning, a policeman in a dark blue uniform saw Sam in the park.

Now use these words to fill the gaps:
some – something – anywhere – anyone

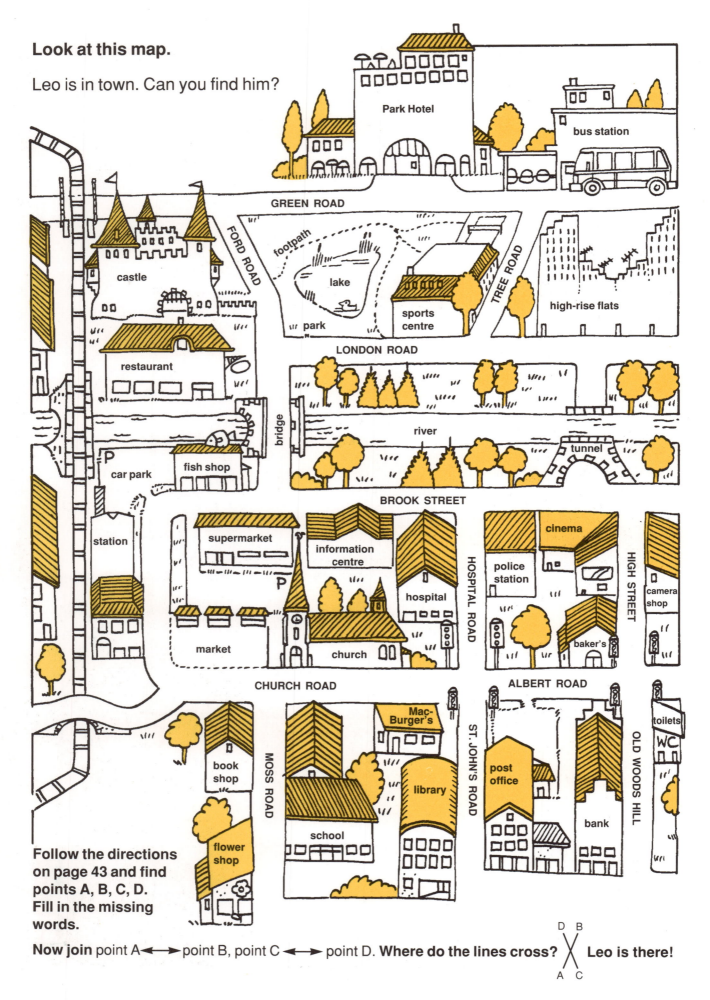

START at the bus station. Take the first turning on the left into [____] Road. Go straight to the end of this road, past the [____] centre, and turn left. Follow this road until you see some high-rise [____] on the left. Opposite the flats there is a [____] under the river. Go through this and turn right into [____] Street. Walk along this street until you see the [____] station at the corner. Now turn [____] and go straight on to the traffic lights. Turn [____] into Church Road. Go past MacBurger's and the church and take the next turning on the left. Go into the [____] shop. It is opposite the school. Look for something to read. This is POINT A.

✹✹✹

START at the supermarket. It is in [____] Street. Cross the river at the first bridge. Go along this [____] until you see the park on the [____]. Walk into the park and follow the footpath round the [____] to the sports [____]. There is a tree on the [____]. This is POINT B.

✹✹✹

START at the bank. Do not walk towards the baker's or the toilets. Turn [____] into St. John's Road. Turn left at the traffic [____]. You are now in [____] Road. There is a [____] on the right. Take the second turning on the left. Stand on the bridge and look at the railway lines. You can see another bridge straight ahead. The middle of this bridge is POINT C.

✹✹✹

START at the castle. Walk to the road and turn right. Go across the [____] and turn [____]. Go past the fish shop and the [____]. Now you can see the [____] on the left. At the second [____] lights look for a food shop. The door is POINT D.

Now can you find Leo?
Leo is at the _____.

Now you try.
Write some directions for a friend.
Tell her or him where to start.

Neue Ensslin-Englischspiele 2

The haunted castle

Das Spukschloß

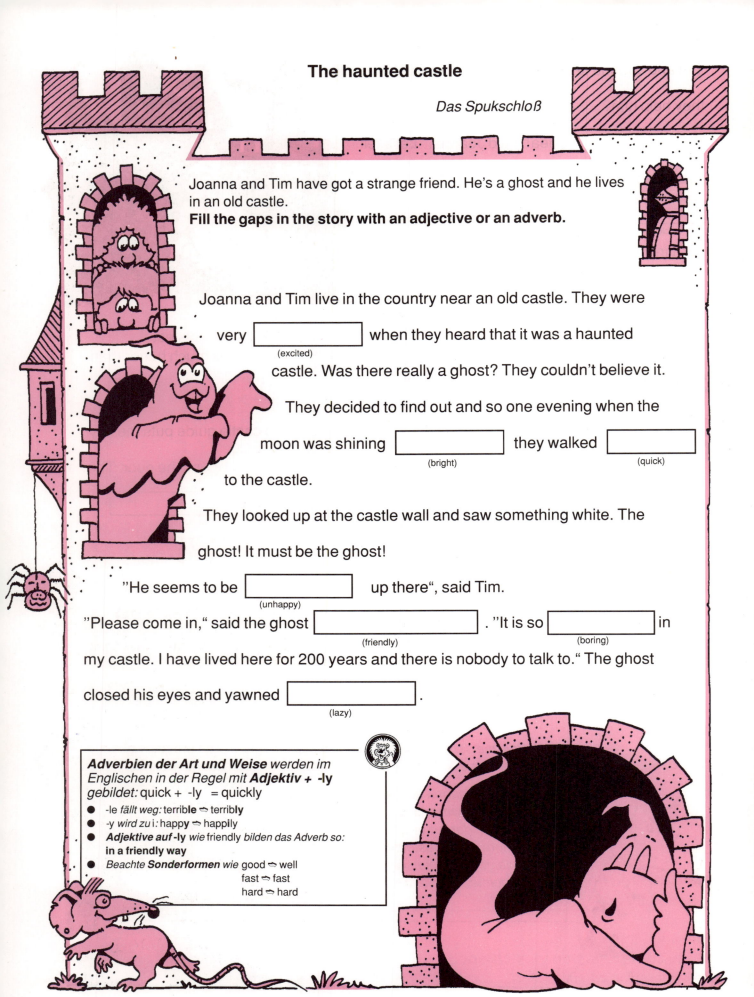

Joanna and Tim have got a strange friend. He's a ghost and he lives in an old castle.
Fill the gaps in the story with an adjective or an adverb.

Joanna and Tim live in the country near an old castle. They were very ☐ (excited) when they heard that it was a haunted castle. Was there really a ghost? They couldn't believe it.

They decided to find out and so one evening when the moon was shining ☐ (bright) they walked ☐ (quick) to the castle.

They looked up at the castle wall and saw something white. The ghost! It must be the ghost!

"He seems to be ☐ (unhappy) up there", said Tim.

"Please come in," said the ghost ☐ (friendly). "It is so ☐ (boring) in my castle. I have lived here for 200 years and there is nobody to talk to." The ghost closed his eyes and yawned ☐ (lazy).

Adverbien der Art und Weise werden im Englischen in der Regel mit **Adjektiv + -ly** gebildet: quick + -ly = quickly
- -le *fällt weg:* terri**ble** ⇨ terri**bly**
- -y *wird zu* i: happ**y** ⇨ happ**i**ly
- **Adjektive auf -ly** *wie* friendly *bilden das Adverb so:* **in a friendly way**
- *Beachte* **Sonderformen** *wie* good ⇨ well
  fast ⇨ fast
  hard ⇨ hard

Tim and Joanna felt sorry for the old ghost. How could they help him?

"I've got a [____] (good) idea!" said Joanna. "Let's tell people about the ghost."

[____] (quick) they made a signpost and put it in the castle gardens.

Then they wrote: "He's the noisiest poltergeist in England! This castle is much better than the Tower of London!"

Now lots of tourists visit the haunted castle. The castle guide puts the key into the lock [____] (careful) and [____] (quiet) opens the door. The tourists go in [____] (nervous). They want to see the [____] (famous) ghost [____] (immediate). The guide calls the old ghost, but today he is [____] (angry). There are too many [____] (noisy) tourists. The tourists are [____] (terrible) [____] (unhappy). They must now drive very [____] (fast) to the next haunted castle! The guide tells them, "That was the worst trick that a ghost can play."

- **Adjektive** sagen aus, **wie jemand oder etwas ist:** an unhappy ghost
- Adjektive stehen vor einem Substantiv oder nach dem Verb *to be*.

- **Adverbien** sagen aus, **wie etwas getan wird:**
  The ghost **yawned lazily**.
- Adverbien der Art und Weise auf **-ly** werden durch Voranstellen von *more/most* gesteigert: more angrily/most angrily
- Einsilbige Adverbien werden mit -er/-est gesteigert: fast/faster/fastest.
- Unregelmäßige Steigerungsformen: well ⇨ better ⇨ best
  badly ⇨ worse ⇨ worst

Neue Ensslin-Englischspiele 2

Leo is making plans for this year

In January **I'm going to visit** my friends in Africa.

In May **I'm going to buy** a new mountain bike.

In September **I'm going to have** a big birthday party.

Look at Leo's plans for this week. Can you finish the sentences?

I'm ____ ____ ____ ____ my ____ ____ ____ .
(clean/bike/tomorrow)

I'm ____ ____ ____ ____ football ____ ____ .
(play/football/this afternoon)

____ ____ ____ to ____ ____ on ____ .
(go climbing/on Saturday)

____ not ____ ____ a ____ at ____ ____ ____ ____ .
(not/see/film/cinema/this week)

Can you ask the questions? Use "going to".

Are ____ ____ ?

Yes, I'm going to go to the post office.

____ ____ ?

Yes, I'm going to learn Spanish at school.

---

*Wenn du über etwas sprichst, was jemand in der Zukunft **fest vorhat**, verwendest du* **to be going to do something**.
I'm going to visit my friends: *Ich werde meine Freunde besuchen.*
I'm not going to play football: *Ich werde nicht Fußball spielen.*
Are you going to buy a CD? *Wirst du eine CD kaufen?*

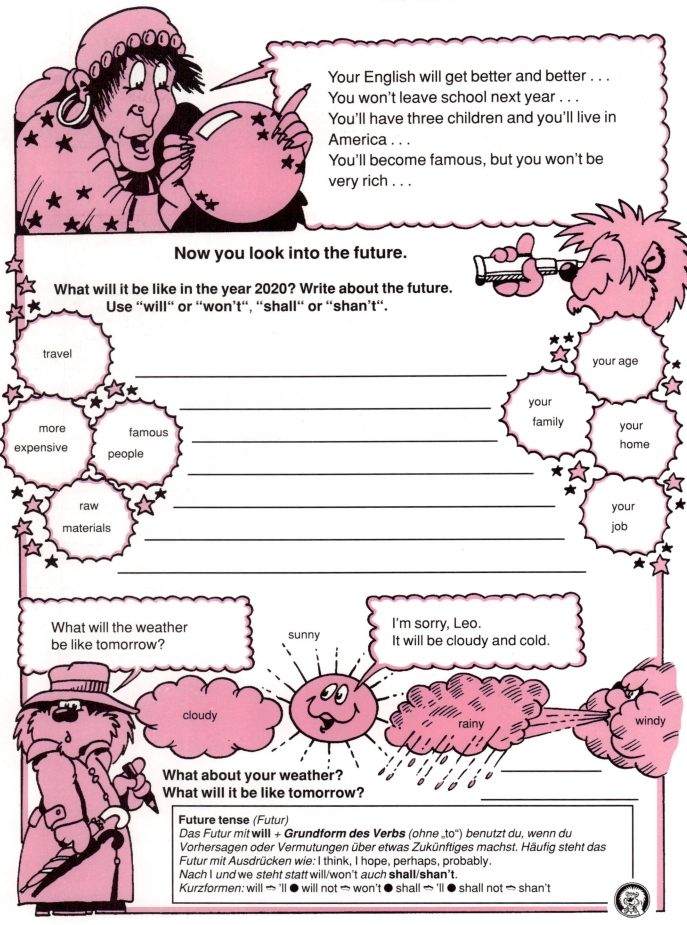

What will happen to the rain forest?

Fill the gaps with the future tense of these verbs:
make – lose – become – (not) grow – wash away – use – grow – cut down.

Workmen _____ the trees.

Millions of animals _____ their homes.

Carpenters _____ the wood into furniture.

Farmers _____ the land for animals.

Rain _____ the soil.

Grass _____ without soil.

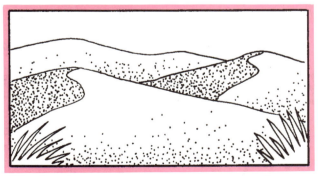

The land _____ a desert and nothing _____

Christmas traditions

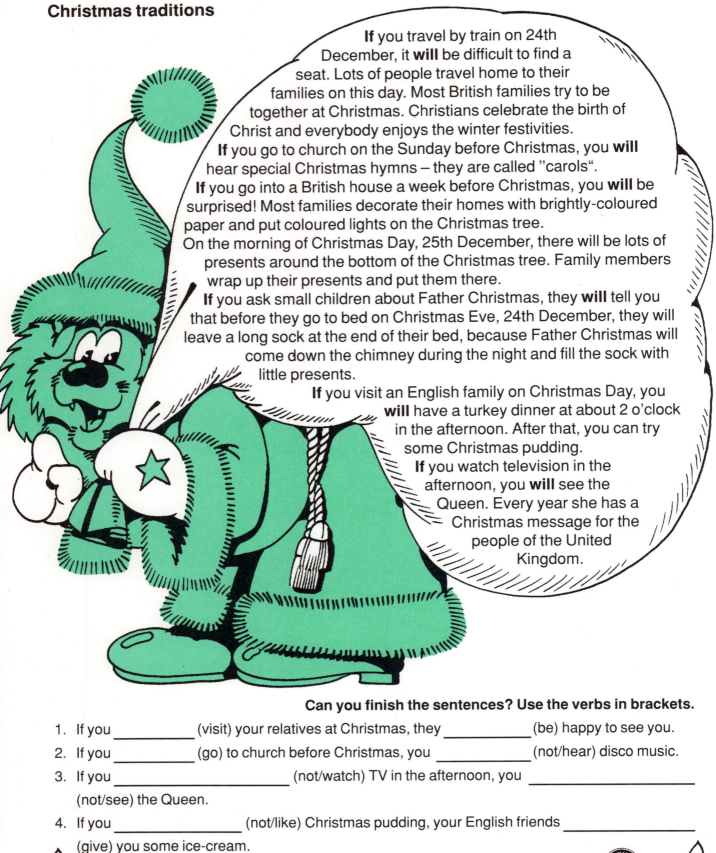

If you travel by train on 24th December, it **will** be difficult to find a seat. Lots of people travel home to their families on this day. Most British families try to be together at Christmas. Christians celebrate the birth of Christ and everybody enjoys the winter festivities.
If you go to church on the Sunday before Christmas, you **will** hear special Christmas hymns – they are called "carols".
If you go into a British house a week before Christmas, you **will** be surprised! Most families decorate their homes with brightly-coloured paper and put coloured lights on the Christmas tree.
On the morning of Christmas Day, 25th December, there will be lots of presents around the bottom of the Christmas tree. Family members wrap up their presents and put them there.
If you ask small children about Father Christmas, they **will** tell you that before they go to bed on Christmas Eve, 24th December, they will leave a long sock at the end of their bed, because Father Christmas will come down the chimney during the night and fill the sock with little presents.
If you visit an English family on Christmas Day, you **will** have a turkey dinner at about 2 o'clock in the afternoon. After that, you can try some Christmas pudding.
If you watch television in the afternoon, you **will** see the Queen. Every year she has a Christmas message for the people of the United Kingdom.

Can you finish the sentences? Use the verbs in brackets.

1. If you _____ (visit) your relatives at Christmas, they _____ (be) happy to see you.
2. If you _____ (go) to church before Christmas, you _____ (not/hear) disco music.
3. If you _____ (not/watch) TV in the afternoon, you _____ (not/see) the Queen.
4. If you _____ (not/like) Christmas pudding, your English friends _____ (give) you some ice-cream.

if bedeutet wenn/falls. Im **Nebensatz** mit **if** steht das **present simple**. Im **Hauptsatz** steht in der Regel **future tense** mit **will**.
If you **travel** by train on 24th December, it **will be difficult** to find a seat.

What happened to Helen's letter?

Beim Abschreiben sind alle Zeilen in Helens Brief durcheinandergeraten. **Findest du die richtige Reihenfolge? Setze auch die fehlenden Possessivbegleiter ein:** my – your – his – her – its – our – their

I	drink _____ milk.
G	afternoon, because _____ French teacher is ill. She
A	John and Mike Baker. They were in the road in front of _____
B	Dear Mary,
E	Helen
C	Love,
K	kitten yesterday! It's lovely, but it doesn't always
A	_____ driving test last week, so I hope we can
A	now. _____ French vocabulary book is waiting for me – ha! ha!
U	Thank you for _____ letter. Listen to
N	We didn't have a French lesson this
M	house. She said they had no lights on _____ bikes. But I
C	this – _____ neighbours gave us a baby
P	think she needs new glasses! _____ brother passed
L	visit you in the Christmas holidays. I must finish
H	fell off _____ bike yesterday evening. She crashed into

Trage die richtige Reihenfolge der Zeilen hier ein:

Do you know who lives here?

_____

Make a snack – a club sandwich

What you need for each sandwich:

* 3 slices of white bread
* 50 g of butter
* 1 small tomato in slices
* 2 small lettuce leaves
* 2 thin slices of ham
* 2 thin slices of cooked chicken or turkey meat
* 1 spoonful of mayonnaise (only if you like it)
* salt and pepper
* 2 party cocktail sticks

What you do:
Toast the bread and cut off the crusts. Put butter on one side of two slices and on both sides of one slice.
Put one slice of toast on a plate (butter on top side) and cover it with the slices of tomato. Season with a little salt and pepper. Then cover the tomato with the ham. Put the slice of toast with butter on both sides on top, and cover it with the lettuce leaves. Season lettuce with a little salt and pepper.
Now cover the lettuce with the cooked chicken or turkey. If you like mayonnaise, spread a spoonful on top. Put the last slice of toast on top. Press the sandwich together carefully! Cut the sandwich in half and stick a party cocktail stick through each half.

Now make some more club sandwiches for your friends.

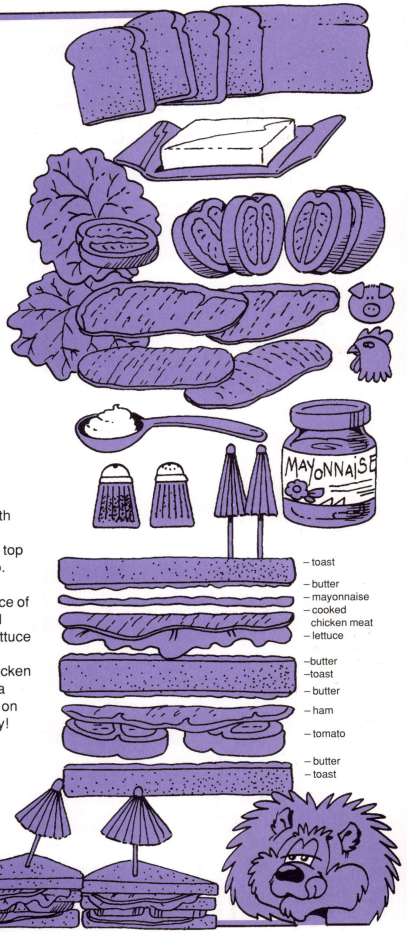

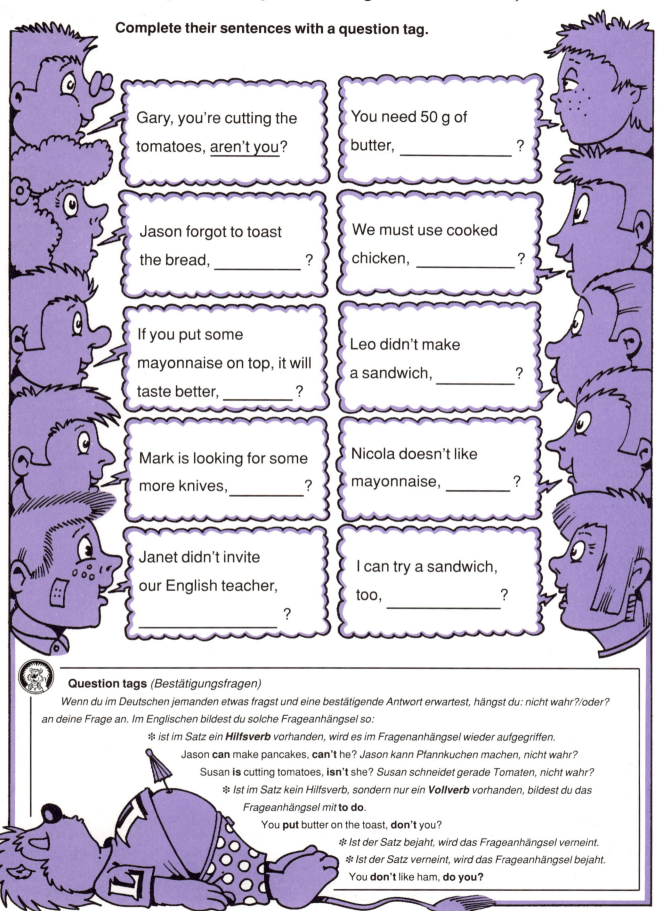

In England people don't celebrate *"Fasching"* or *"Karneval"*. But they sometimes go to fancy dress balls. Look at Jason and Olivia. They are wearing "fancy dress", but their clothes don't fit!

Jason's waistcoat is too tight. The sleeves of his shirt aren't long enough. His trousers are too long. His shoes are too big. But Jason likes these clothes!

fancy dress ball: *Maskenball*
waistcoat: *Weste*

hat/not big enough

earrings/too big

sleeves/too long

Now write about Olivia's clothes.

skirt/too tight

boots/too small

_____
_____
_____
_____
_____

What about your clothes? Do they all fit?
_____
_____

Wörter wie **trousers, jeans, shorts, pants, tights, clothes** stehen **immer in der Mehrzahlform**. Bei „Beinkleidern" wird die Einzahl zum Beispiel so ausgedrückt: eine Hose = **a pair of** trousers.

Your clothes page

What are your favourite clothes? *I like* _____
_____ *best.*

What new clothes do you need? *I need* _____
_____

What clothes do you wear at school? _____
_____

Where would you like to go for a week's holiday? *I would like to go to* _____
_____

What would you like to do there? *I would like to* _____
_____

A clothes quiz

Wear these in summer when it's too hot for jeans. → ○ _ _ _ _ _ _ _

It's something to put on your head. → ○ _ _ _

Wear this over a shirt. → ○ _ _ _ _ _ _ _

A boy or a man puts this round his neck. → ○ _ _ _

Wear these on your feet at home. → ○ _ _ _ _ _ _

Lösungswort: ○○○○○

Now pack your holiday case.

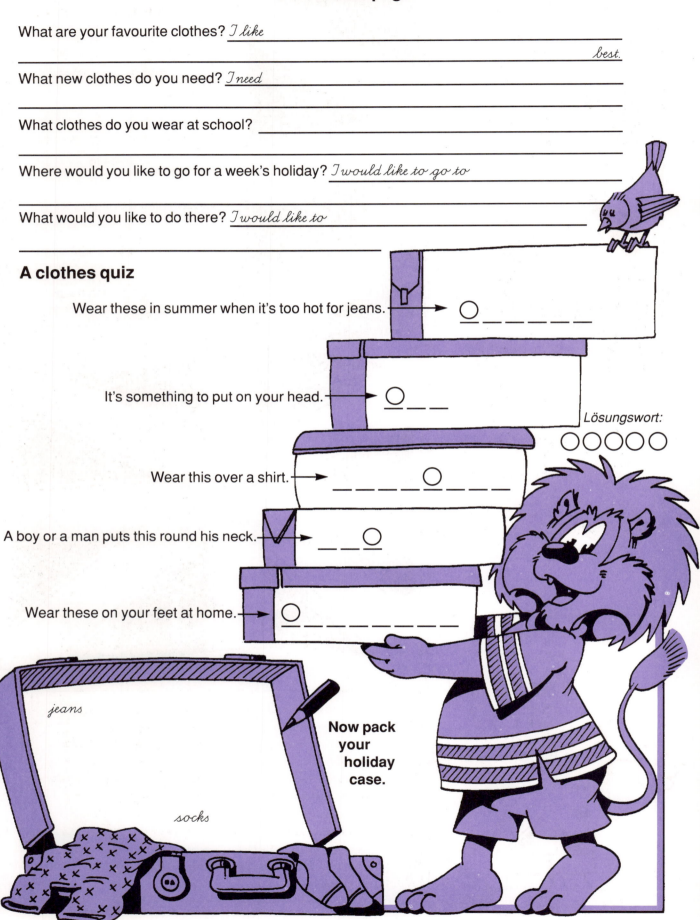

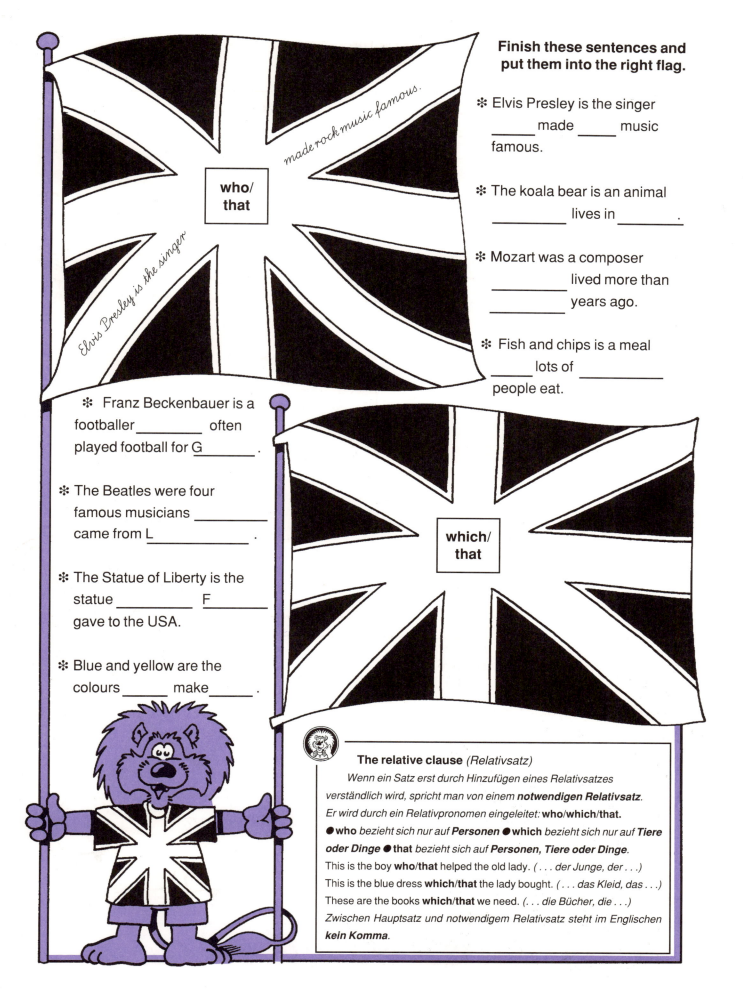

Strange Traditions

Do you know what happens in England on New Year's Eve? You certainly won't see any fireworks! People who live in London often go to Trafalgar Square and lots of young people jump into the fountain there at midnight!
In other towns crowds gather in the main squares to sing and dance and "see the New Year in".
There are special services in churches everywhere.
Now you may think that the British hate fireworks. Of course, this isn't true. There is one night in the year when the British celebrate with bonfires and fireworks. This night has a long tradition and here is the story:
In 1605, King James I was King of England. The Roman Catholics in England didn't like him because he was a Protestant. That year King James had to open Parliament on 5th November. Some Catholics planned to blow up the Houses of Parliament. So on the night of 4th November they hid 36 barrels of gunpowder under the House of Lords. They chose a man called Guy Fawkes to explode the barrels. However, the King heard about these plans and his men found Guy Fawkes and arrested him. Later, the King ordered his men to hang Guy Fawkes and the other conspirators.
Since 1605, on the first day of a new Parliament, guards called *Beefeaters* still search the cellars of the House of Commons and the House of Lords before the members of Parliament arrive. Of course, they don't really expect to find barrels of gunpowder!
In England, people call November 5th "Bonfire Night". Weeks before, children collect wood for a bonfire in their garden. Then they make a dummy – a "guy" like Guy Fawkes – from old clothes, which they fill with straw or newspaper. In towns, children often sit on the pavement with their "guy" and ask passers-by to give them "a penny for the guy". They buy fireworks with the money they collect.
On the evening of 5th November the family stands round the bonfire. They put the guy on top. Then the parents light the bonfire and the family chants: "Remember, remember the Fifth of November." Then they let off their fireworks. It can be very cold in November and everyone is pleased to eat the traditional food that their parents have prepared: hot dogs, roasted chestnuts and hot chocolate.

If you don't know some of the words, look at the vocabulary list on page 62.

What did you do on New Year's Eve last year?

_____

_____

_____

What did you have to eat?

I had _____

_____

_____

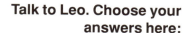
Talk to Leo. Choose your answers here:

 Lots of people think that fireworks are a waste of money. What do you think?

you:

| I agree. I think so, too. |
| I disagree. I don't think so. |
| Sorry, I'm not sure. |

 I think that most animals are afraid of fireworks. What do you think?

you:

 Children mustn't let off fireworks. This is too dangerous. What do you think?

you:

 Would you like to have a bonfire on New Year's Eve?

| Yes, I would. |
| No, I wouldn't. |

you:

 Would you like to go to London and visit the Houses of Parliament?

you:

 What else would you like to see in London?

| I would like to . . . |

you:

Now ask your teacher a few questions.
Your questions: **Your teacher's answers:**

Neue Ensslin-Englischspiele 2

Can you do this bumper crossword?

You can find the words in the text "Strange traditions" on page 58.

across:

1 Children collect "a . . . for the guy".
2 On 5th November there are lots of . . .
3 This is not a box, . . . is a barrel.
4 The opposite of "false" is . . .
5 The family stands . . . the bonfire.
6 The opposite of "closed" is . . .
7 Beer is usually put in this.
8 Another word for "Eve" is . . .
9 Let's go . . . the house.
10 Opposite of "she".
11 Children call their . . . a "guy".
12 A . . . of people go to Trafalgar Square.
13 Something that happens every year is often a . . .
14 Guy Fawkes was a . . .
15 Infinitive form of "said".
16 A number.
17 Lucy isn't . . . home.
18 Past tense of "sit".
19 Animals don't like fireworks; they are . . . of them.
20 To look for = to . . . for.
21 Opposite of "young".
22 The eleventh month.
23 Trafalgar . . .
24 Children fill their "guy" with . . .
25 In winter you can buy roasted . . .
26 Opposite of "short".
27 I often go swimming. I . . . swimming.
28 The conspirators hid it under the House of Lords.
29 Past tense of "go".
30 Not *this* book, . . . book.
31 Opposite of "cold".
32 I haven't got . . . fireworks.
33 Children ask . . . for a penny for the guy.

down:

1 The Queen opens . . . every year.
2 The guards at the House of Commons.
6 The guy is dressed in . . . . . .
29 Past tense of "is".
30 They go . . . Trafalgar Square.
34 Something that is unusual is sometimes . . .
35 . . . are bigger than villages.
36 Is this . . . book?
37 Please don't walk on the road, walk on the . . .
38 King James I wasn't Roman Catholic, he was . . .
39 A lot of people.
40 At the moment.
41 Opposite of "night".
42 On Sunday people go to . . .
43 Past tense of "choose".
44 Children collect money for . . .
45 The guy is on . . . of the bonfire.
46 Past tense of "hear".
47 You can see these at Trafalgar Square.
48 Another word for "therefore".
49 Look at those children! . . . guy is really big.
50 Plural of "is".
51 Present tense of "did".
52 A number.
53 Rooms underneath a building.
54 The new day starts just after . . .

Die englische Aussprache

Du weißt, daß manche Buchstaben im Englischen anders als im Deutschen ausgesprochen werden. Diese Lautschrift hilft dir, Wörter richtig auszusprechen, die du noch nicht kennst.

['] Der Apostroph steht vor der betonten Silbe eines Wortes.
[i:] Zwei Punkte hinter einem Buchstaben der Lautschrift bedeuten, daß du den Buchstaben lang aussprichst. Zum Beispiel: [i:] wie in *tief*: feet [i:].

[ʌ] kurzes *a* fast wie in *Kamm*: cup [kʌp]
[æ] fast wie *ä* in *Säge*, aber mehr zum *a* hin: cat [kʌt]
[ə] wie *e* am Ende von *Berge*: sister [sistə]
[e] wie *e* in *nett*: bed [bed]
[ɜ:] wie *ö* in *Löwe*: circle [sɜ:kl]
[ɪ] wie *i* in *mit*: penguin ['pengwɪn]
[ɒ] wie *o* in *Post*: clock [klɒk]
[ɔ:] wie *o* in *Lord* (aber ohne „*r*"): ball [bɔ:l]
[ʊ] wie *u* in *Bulle*: foot [fʊt]

[eə] wie *ä* in *Bär*: airplane [eəpleɪn]
[ɔɪ] wie *eu* in *neu*: boy [bɔɪ]

[d] + [b] + [g] Diese Buchstaben spricht man im Englischen immer weich aus, so wie in Dachs, Bär und Gans – auch dann, wenn sie am Wortende stehen: red [red].
[r] Das r hört sich im Englischen an wie in „Rock 'n' roll"
[z] wie *s* in *lesen*: blouse [blaʊz]
[ʃ] wie *sch* in *Fisch*: dish [dɪʃ]
[ʒ] wie *g* in *Etage*: television [telɪvɪʒn]
[dʒ] wie *J* in *Job*: bridge [brɪdʒ]
[θ] wie *ß* in *Baß*, aber gelispelt: things [θɪŋgz]
[ð] wie *s* in *Sense*, aber gelispelt: with [wɪð]
[v] wie im Deutschen in *Vase*: very ['verɪ]
[w] sehr kurzes *u* – kein deutsches *w*: window ['wɪndoʊ]

• •

Alphabetisches Wörterverzeichnis

a few [fjuː]	ein paar
absurd [əb'sɜːd]	absurd, abwegig
accident ['æksɪdənt]	Unfall
across	(quer) über
to add	dazugeben
to agree	übereinstimmen
along	entlang
always	immer
angry	ärgerlich
area ['eərɪə]	Gebiet
to arrest	verhaften
Austria ['ɒstrɪə]	Österreich
baker's	Bäckerei
barbecue ['baːbɪkjuː]	Grillfest
barrel	Faß
bathing costume	Badeanzug
bathing trunks	Badehose
bathroom	Badezimmer
to be afraid of [ə'freɪd]	Angst haben vor
to be dressed in	bekleidet sein mit
to beat [biːt], beat, beaten	schlagen, aufschlagen
to become [bɪ'kʌm], became, become	werden
Belgium ['beldʒəm]	Belgien
to believe [bɪ'liːv]	glauben
bike	Fahrrad
birth	Geburt
biscuit ['bɪskɪt]	Keks
bo bite [baɪt], bit [bɪt], bitten	beißen
blouse [blaʊz]	Bluse
to blow up [bloʊ], blew, blown	*hier:* in die Luft sprengen
bone [boʊn]	Knochen
bonfire	Freudenfeuer
boots [buːts]	Stiefel
boring ['bɔːrɪŋ]	langweilig
brain [breɪn]	Gehirn
to break [breɪk], broke [broʊk], broken	brechen
bridge [brɪdʒ]	Brücke
bright [braɪt]	hell, leuchtend
to build [bɪld], built, built	bauen
building	Gebäude
bumper crossword	Riesenkreuzworträtsel
bus station	Busbahnhof
butterfly	Schmetterling
cage [keɪdʒ]	Käfig
cake [keɪk]	Kuchen
camera shop	Fotogeschäft
camper	Wohnmobil
campsite ['kæmpsaɪt]	Zeltplatz
careful ['keəfʊl]	vorsichtig
carol ['kærəl]	Weihnachtslied
carpenter	Zimmermann, Tischler
case [keɪs]	Koffer
castle [kaːsl]	Burg, Schloß
ceiling ['siːlɪŋ]	Zimmerdecke
to celebrate ['selɪbreɪt]	feiern
cellar ['selə]	Keller
certainly ['sɜːtnlɪ]	gewiß, sicherlich
shamrock	Kleeblatt
to chant	singen
to chase ['tʃeɪs]	jagen
cheetah ['tʃiːtə]	Gepard
chimney	Kamin, Schornstein
chocolate	Schokolade
to choose [tʃuːz], chose, chosen	(aus)wählen
Christ ['kraɪst]	Jesus Christus
Christian ['krɪstjən]	Christ(in); christlich
Christmas	Weihnachten
Christmas pudding	Plumpudding
circus workshop	Werkstattzirkus
cinema ['sɪnɪmə]	Kino
clever	klug
climber ['klaɪmə]	Kletterer
cloudy ['klaʊdɪ]	wolkig
coast [koʊst]	Küste
coat	Mantel
cocktail stick	Cocktailstäbchen
cocoa ['koʊkoʊ]	Kakao
to collect	sammeln
colour	Farbe
to compare [kəm'peə]	vergleichen
to complete	vervollständigen
composer	Komponist
conspirator	Verschwörer
cooked chicken meat	Hühnchenaufschnitt
could [kʊd]	konnte, könnte
country ['kʌntrɪ]	Land
cow [kaʊ]	Kuh
to crash into	zusammenstoßen mit, krachen gegen
to cross	überqueren
crust	Kruste
to cut, cut, cut	schneiden
daffodil	Märzenbecher, Narzisse
dangerous ['deɪndʒərəs]	gefährlich
dead [ded]	tot
to decide [dɪ'saɪd]	entscheiden
desert ['dezət]	Wüste
to die [daɪ], died, died	sterben
difficult	schwierig
direction [dɪ'rekʃn]	Richtung
directions	Anweisungen
to disagree	nicht übereinstimmen mit
to do the washing-up	abspülen
to do, did, done	machen, tun
double bass [dʌbl beɪs]	Kontrabass
dress	Kleid
to drink, drank, drunk	trinken
driving test	Fahrprüfung
dummy ['dʌmɪ]	Attrappe, Puppe
early ['ɜːlɪ]	früh
earth [ɜːθ]	Erde
earthquake ['ɜːθkweɪk]	Erdbeben
Easter ['iːstə]	Ostern
to eat, ate, eaten	essen

to enjoy [ɪn'dʒɔɪ]	genießen
enough [ɪ'nʌf]	genug
equipment [ɪ'kwɪpmənt]	*hier:* Küchengeräte
everybody	alle, jeder, jede, jedes
everywhere	überall
excited [ɪ'ksaɪtɪd]	aufgeregt
to expect	erwarten
expensive	teuer
to fall off, fell, fallen	abstürzen
famous	berühmt
fancy that	stell dir vor!
favourite	Lieblings-
to feed, fed, fed	füttern
to feel, felt, felt	(sich) fühlen
to feel sorry for	Mitleid mit jemandem haben
festivity	Festlichkeit
to fetch	(her)holen
fierce [fɪəs]	wild
to find, found, found	finden
to find out	herausfinden
to finish	beenden, fertigmachen
fireworks	Feuerwerk
fish and chips	in Backteig ausgebratener Fisch und Pommes frites
to fit, fit, fit	passen
flag	Flagge
flour ['flauə]	Mehl
fly [flaɪ]	Fliege
fog	Nebel
to follow ['fɒləu]	(be)folgen
food	Essen
footpath	Fußweg
to forget, forgot, forgotten	vergessen
fountain	Springbrunnen
France [fra:ns]	Frankreich
French	französisch
to fry	(in der Pfanne) braten
furniture ['fɜ:nɪtʃə]	Möbel
future ['fju:tʃə]	Zukunft
gap	Lücke
to gather	sammeln
to get up, got, got	aufstehen
ghost [gəust]	Geist
to give, gave, given	geben
to go, went, gone	gehen, fahren
to go on a bike tour	eine Fahrradtour machen
to go riding	reiten gehen
to go sightseeing ['saɪtsi:ɪŋ]	Sehenswürdigkeiten ansehen
Greece [gri:s]	Griechenland
guard [ga:d]	Wache
gunpowder ['gʌnpaʊdə]	Schießpulver
(he) had to	(er) mußte
ham	Schinken
to happen	geschehen
to hate [heɪt]	hassen
haunted castle [hɔ:ntɪd . . .]	Spukschloß
to have, had, had	haben
to hear, heard, heard	hören
heavy	schwer
to help	helfen
hidden word	verstecktes Wort
to hide, hid, hidden	verstecken
high-rise flats ['haɪraɪs . . .]	Wohnblock, Hochhaus
hog	Wildschwein
to hold [həʊld], held, held	halten
hole [həʊl]	Loch
hostel	*hier:* Obdachlosenheim
House of Commons	Unterhaus
House of Lords	Oberhaus
Houses of Parliament [. . . pa:ləmənt]	Ober- und Unterhaus des britischen Parlaments
how [haʊ]	wie
however [haʊ'evə]	jedoch
hutch [hʌtʃ]	Kaninchenstall
hymn [hɪm]	Kirchenlied
ill	krank

immediately [ɪ'mɪdjətlɪ]	sofort
in the country	auf dem Land
ingredients [ɪn'gri:djənts]	Zutaten
to invite [ɪn'vaɪt]	einladen
irregular	unregelmäßig
Italy ['ɪtəlɪ]	Italien
to jiggle ['dʒɪgl]	zappeln
to join [dʒɔɪn]	verbinden
to keep warm, kept, kept	(sich) warm halten
key	Schlüssel
kind [kaɪnd]	liebenswürdig
kitchen	Küche
kitten	Kätzchen
to know, knew, known	wissen, kennen
ladder	Leiter
lady	Dame
lazy ['leɪzɪ]	faul
to leave, left, left	(ver)lassen
lemon juice [. . . dʒu:s]	Zitronensaft
to let off fireworks, let, let	Feuerwerkskörper abschießen
lettuce leaf ['letɪs 'li:f]	Salatblatt
library ['laɪbrərɪ]	Bücherei
to lock	zusperren
lorry ['lɒrɪ]	Lastwagen
to lose [lu:z], lost, lost	verlieren
lunch	Mittagessen
lunch break	Mittagspause
main [meɪn]	Haupt-
to make, made, made	machen, tun
meal [mi:l]	Essen, Mahlzeit
to meet [mi:t], met, met	treffen
member	Mitglied
message ['mesɪdʒ]	Botschaft
midnight	Mitternacht
missing	fehlend
mixing bowl [. . . bəul]	Rührschüssel
monkey	Affe
mountain rescue team	Gebirgsrettungsmannschaft
mushroom	Champignon
musician [mju:'zɪʃn]	Musiker
naughty ['nɔ:tɪ]	frech
near	in der Nähe
neck	Hals
necklace ['neklɪs]	Halskette
to need	brauchen
nervous ['nɜ:vəs]	nervös
never	nie, niemals
New Year's Eve [. . . i:v]	Silvester
news	Nachrichten
newspaper	Zeitung
night-dress	Nachthemd
non-stick frying pan	beschichtete Bratpfanne
of course	natürlich
oil [ɔɪl]	Öl
on top	obendrauf
onion ['ʌnjən]	Zwiebel
opposite	gegenüber; Gegenteil
orange juice [. . . dʒu:s]	Orangensaft
organ ['ɔ:gən]	Orgel
over	über
own	eigener, eigene, eigenes
to pack	packen
to paint	anstreichen, malen
pants	Unterhose
parents	Eltern
part	Teil
passer-by	Passant
past	vorbei an
path	Fußweg
pavement ['peɪvmənt]	Gehsteig
pepper	Pfeffer
pet	Haustier
to pick flowers	Blumen pflücken
picture	Bild
plant	Pflanze
plate [pleɪt]	Teller

Neue Ensslin-Englischspiele 2

pleased [pli:zd]	erfreut	to speak, spoke, spoken	sprechen
poetry	Poesie, Gedichte	spider [spaɪdə]	Spinne
point	Punkt	to spread [spred]	verteilen
police station	Polizeiwache	square [skweə]	(öffentlicher) Platz
policeman	Polizist	statue [stætʃu:]	Statue
post office	Postamt	to stay	bleiben; wohnen
to pour [pɔ:]	gießen	to steal [sti:l], stole, stolen	stehlen
to practise	üben	to stick in	einkleben
to prepare	vorbereiten	to stick through [...θru:]	durchstecken
present	Geschenk	stove [stəʊv]	Herd
to press	drücken	straight (ahead) [streɪt]	gerade(aus)
pretty [prɪtɪ]	hübsch	strange [streɪndʒ]	komisch, merkwürdig
pupil	Schüler	straw [strɔ:]	Stroh
pyjamas [pə'dʒa:məz]	Schlafanzug	sure [ʃʊə]	sicher
python [paɪθn]	Pythonschlange; Riesenschlange	surprised [sə'praɪzd]	überrascht
question	Frage	to swallow [swɒləʊ]	schlucken
race [reɪs]	Rennen	to swim, swam, swum	schwimmen
railway lines	Eisenbahnschienen	to take, took, taken	nehmen
rain	Regen	tall [tɔ:l]	groß, hochgewachsen
rain forest	Regenwald	team	Mannschaft
raw materials [rɔ:...]	Rohstoffe	to test	prüfen
to read, read, read [ri:d, red, red]	lesen	therefore	deshalb
real	echt	thick	dick
really	wirklich	to think, thought, thought	denken
reason	Grund	thistle [θɪsl]	Distel
Red Cross	Rotes Kreuz	through	durch
relatives	Verwandte	ticket	(Eintritts-)Karte
to remember	sich erinnern an	to tickle [tɪkl]	kitzeln
reply [rɪ'plaɪ]	Antwort	tie [taɪ]	Krawatte
to reply	beantworten	tight [taɪt]	eng
reporter	Berichterstatter	tights	Strumpfhose
rhyme [raɪm]	Reim	together	zusammen
right order	richtige Reihenfolge	toilets	Toiletten
roasted chestnuts [rəʊstɪd...]	heiße Maronen	to toss	werfen
robber	Räuber	towards	auf...zu
to roll up [rəʊl...]	aufrollen	town	Stadt
to roller-skate	Rollschuh fahren	traditional	traditionell
Roman Catholic	Katholik(in)	Trafalgar Square	*berühmter Platz in London*
roof	Dach	traffic lights	Verkehrsampel
room	Zimmer, Raum	train	Zug
to run, ran, run	rennen	trainers	Turnschuhe
salt [sɔ:lt]	Salz	to travel	reisen
sandals	Sandalen	trousers	Hose
to save [seɪv]	*hier:* retten	to try	versuchen
scarf	Schal	turkey	Truthahn
school uniform [...'ju:nɪfɔ:m]	Schuluniform	turning	Straßenbiegung, Abzweigung
sea [si:]	Meer	underneath	unter
to search for [sɜ:tʃ]	suchen nach	United Kingdom	Vereinigtes Königreich (England, Schottland, Wales und Nordirland)
to season [si:zn]	*hier:* würzen		
seat [si:t]	Sitz		
to see, saw, seen	sehen	to use	benutzen
"to see the New Year in"	Neujahr feiern	usually	normalerweise
to seem	(zu sein) scheinen	vest	Unterhemd
sentence	Satz	visitor	Besucher
service	Leistung	vocabulary book	Vokabelheft
to shake, shook, shaken	schütteln	waistcoat ['weɪskəʊt]	Weste
shed	Geräteschuppen	to wait	warten
shelter	Schutz	wall [wɔ:l]	Mauer
to shine, shone, shone	scheinen, leuchten	to wash away	wegspülen
shirt	Hemd	waste of money [weɪst]	Geldverschwendung
shorts	kurze Hose	to watch TV	fernsehen
to sieve [sɪv]	durchsieben	to wear, wore, worn	tragen (von Kleidung)
signpost ['saɪnpəʊst]	(Straßen-)Schild, Wegweiser	to weigh [weɪ]	wiegen
since	seit	well-known	bekannt
to sit, sat, sat	sitzen	whale [weɪl]	Wal
skirt	Rock	what else?	was noch?
sleeve [sli:v]	Ärmel	whisk [wɪsk]	Schneebesen
slice [slaɪs]	Scheibe	why [waɪ]	warum
slippers	Hausschuhe	to win, won, won	gewinnen
to smile [smaɪl]	lächeln	without	ohne
to smoke [sməʊk]	rauchen	wood [wʊd]	Holz
snack	Imbiß	world [wɜ:ld]	Welt
soil [sɔɪl]	Erde	to wrap up [ræp]	einpacken
sometimes	manchmal	to wriggle [rɪgl]	zappeln
Spain [speɪn]	Spanien	to write [raɪt], wrote, written	schreiben
Spanish	spanisch	to yawn [jɔ:n]	gähnen

Lösungen:

page 3: LEO AND LUCY   **page 6:** *Lösungswort:* school uniform

page 7: I get up at seven o'clock. I put on my school uniform. Then I have breakfast. I have corn-flakes and toast and jam. I have a cup of tea. I go to school at half past eight. My mother takes me to school by car. School starts at 8.50. I have a sandwich for lunch. My last lesson finishes at four o'clock. After dinner I do my homework. Then I play table tennis with my brother.

page 9: He doesn't feel hungry / Do you want / I don't think / Does your teacher / I dont' know / Why do you ask? / How does Mother know / Do you want / Peter doesn't like the idea. – two thistles from Scotland.

page 10: hobbies, skirts, shoes, pens, feet, pets, teeth, keys, children, roses, ponies, cows, apples, churches, boys, sandwiches, knives, mice, tomatoes, men, newspapers, fish, women, sausages; Leo says: Plural words are very easy.

page 11: I usually have breakfast in the kitchen at seven o'clock. I often do my homework in my room after dinner. I sometimes go to the table tennis club after school.

page 12: Jim is phoning Kevin. Father is working in the garden. They are dancing. Lucy is cleaning her bike. Mother is reading a book. Mac is sleeping. Fluff is chasing a mouse. – What are they building? Well, they are not building a school. Which book is mother reading? Well, she isn't reading her poetry book.

page 13: 1) Dad, some monkeys are sitting on our car. They often jump onto cars. 2) Look, they are going to the next car now. 3) Help! What is that elephant doing? 4) It is looking for an apple. 5) Do tourists often feed the animals? 6) Why is that wolf hiding behind a tree? A lot of animals don't like visitors. 7) That giraffe is watching us. It looks hungry. But giraffes never eat people. 8) These lions are waiting for their food. 9) Do zebras like picnics, too?

page 15: lose – lost, is – was, spend – spent, send – sent, leave – left, are – were, help – helped, find – found, die – died. The team helped climbers in Wales. When did the climbers leave? No, they didn't know their way. Where did they spend the night?

page 17: Great Britain, Belgium, Germany, Austria, Italy, Spain, Portugal, France. 1) helped, 2) left, 3) took, 4) sent, 5) saw / 5) spent, 6) lost, 7) were, 8) found, 9) was, 10) liked. The hidden word is: Europe.

page 19: She swallowed the cat to catch the bird to catch the spider that wriggled and jiggled and tickled inside her. She swallowed the spider to catch the fly. I don't know why she swallowed a fly. Perhaps she'll die. There was an old lady who swallowed a cow. I don't know how, but she swallowed a cow! There was an old lady who swallowed a horse.

page 22: my parents' car, the tigers' cages, the dog's bone, John's snowboard, the roof of the house, my mother's ring, the men's hats

page 23: better, faster, prettier, smaller, happier, taller

page 25: A butterfly is more beautiful than a spider. A spider is not as beautiful as a butterfly. A tuba is heavier than a trumpet. A trumpet is not as heavy as a tuba. A lion is more dangerous than a cat. A double bass is not as small as a violin.

page 26: highest, hottest, longest; most expensive, most famous, most difficult, most dangerous

page 27: At 11 o'clock he was playing football. At 12.15 he was having lunch. At 1 o'clock he was listening to CDs. At 2.30 he was cleaning his rabbit's hutch. At 3.45 he was writing a letter to his pen-friend. – Mother was reading a book, when the telephone rang. Jo fell off the ladder while he was painting the kitchen ceiling. We were waiting for the bus when we saw an accident.

page 29: Jim has lost his key. Anita has broken her arm. Mrs. Brown has had a baby. Tom and Ann have gone to America. David has opened the window. Susan has posted a letter. Jill and Jack have finished breakfast. John has cleaned his shoes.

Ich habe diese Karte aus dem Heft:
Englischspiele Band 2

○ Dieses Heft war ein Geschenk.
○ Ich habe es mir selbst ausgesucht / gekauft. (Wo?)

....

An / in diesem Heft gefällt mir:

....

....

Das finde ich nicht gut:

....

....

Ich bin . . . Jahre alt. Meine Hobbys / Interessen:

....

....

○ Ich möchte wissen, was der Ensslin-Verlag sonst noch macht. Bitte schickt mir kostenloses Prospektmaterial zu. Diese Karte geht an:

**Ensslin-Verlag
Postfach 15 32
D-72705 Reutlingen**

Jeder 50. Einsender erhält zusätzlich ein tolles Buchgeschenk.

page 30: I have just helped the clowns. I have never held a giant python. I have already played with the monkeys. I haven't seen the acrobats yet. – Have you ever watched ... Have you ever jumped ...

page 31: lose – lost – lost; go – went – gone; have – had – had; feed – fed – fed; do – did – done; sit – sat – sat; win – won – won; give – gave – given; hold – held – held; see – saw – seen

page 32: I have been picking flowers. I have been talking to farmer Elliot. I have been doing the washing-up. I have been fetching water from the farm-house. I have been writing letters. I have been cooking sausages. I have been collecting wood. I have been repairing my bike.

page 33: 1) John has been talking to the newspaper reporter for 10 minutes. 2) The children have been waiting to see the whale go back into the sea since this morning. 3) I have been looking for the other whales since 2 o'clock. 4) Sheila has been talking to the whale for a long time. 5) We have been pouring water over the whale for an hour.

page 36: sugar = Zucker, ingredients = Zutaten, flour = Mehl, sieve = Sieb, frying pan = Bratpfanne, equipment = Gerät (Küchengeräte), smooth = glatt, whisk = Schneebesen

page 37: von links nach rechts: over, into, through, round, across, towards, along, onto, past, after, out of, up

page 38: 1) across, 2) over, 3) into, 4) up, 5) onto, 6) through, 7) past, 8) towards, 9) into, 10) out of, 11) along, 12) round, 13) after

page 40: some, any, somewhere, anything, any, somebody, some, anything

page 41: anywhere – anyone – something – some – some   **page 43:** Leo is at the information centre.

page 44: excited – brightly – quickly – unhappy – in a friendly way – boring – lazily

page 45: good – quickly – carefully – quietly – nervously – famous – immediately – angry – noisy – terribly – unhappy – fast

page 46: I'm going to clean my bike tomorrow. I'm going to go climbing on Saturday. I'm going to play football this afternoon. I'm not going to see a film at the cinema this week. – Are you going to go to the post office? Are you going to learn Spanish at school?

page 47: The dog is going to bite the robber. Tom is going to win the race. It is going to rain soon.

page 49: Workmen will cut down the trees. Millions of animals will lose their homes. Carpenters will make the wood into furniture. Farmers will use the land for animals. Rain will wash away the soil. Grass won't grow without soil. The land will become a desert and nothing will grow.

page 50: 1. If you visit your relatives ..., they will be happy to see you. 2. If you go to church ..., you will not (won't) hear disco music. 3. If you don't watch TV ..., you will not (won't) see the Queen. 4. If you don't like Christmas pudding, your English friends will give you ...

page 51: its milk – our French teacher – in front of her – his driving test – my French vocabulary book – your letter – their bikes – our neighbours – my brother – her bike. BUCKINGHAM PALACE. The Queen lives there.

page 53: You need 50 g of butter, don't you? Jason forgot to toast the bread, didn't he? We must use cooked chicken, mustn't we? ... it will taste better, won't it? Leo didn't make a sandwich, did he? Mark is looking for some more knives, isn't he? Nicola doesn't like mayonnaise, does she? Janet didn't invite our English teacher, did she? I can try a sandwich, too, can't I?

page 56: shorts, hat, pullover, tie, slippers – Lösungwort: shoes

page 57: The koala bear is an animal which/that lives in Australia. Mozart was a composer who/that lived more than 200 years ago. Fish and chips is a meal which/that lots of British people eat. Franz Beckenbauer is a footballer who/that often played football for Germany. The Beatles were four famous musicians who/that came from Liverpool. The Statue of Liberty is the statue which/that France gave to the USA. Blue and yellow are the colours which/that make green.